ELIJAH MUHAMMAD'S
NEW WORLD NATION
OF ISLAM

A.M. MUHAMMAD

NWNOI PUBLICATIONS

New World Nation of Islam Publications
PO Box 8466
Newark, NJ 07108
888-213-2409
Email: truth@newworldnationislam.com
http://www.nwnoi.org

Elijah Muhammad's New World Nation of Islam
by A.M. Muhammad
    Ebook ISBN 13-digit 978-1-957954-15-8
    Paperback ISBN 13-digit 978-1-957954-16-5

    Library of Congress Cataloging-In-Publication Data:

    Library of Congress Control Number: 2022913289

        1. Islam 2. African American 3. Elijah
        Muhammad 4. Messenger of Allah 5. Nation of
        Islam 6. Master Fard Muhammad 7. Black
        Muslims 8. New World Nation of Islam

    Cover design and layout by Nuance Art LLC
    Book design by Nuance Art LLC

DEDICATED TO:

The Most Honorable Mr. Elijah Muhammad The Last God Of The Old World And First God Of The New World Nation Of Islam.

Holy Qur'an Chapter 10 Verse 47:

"And For Every Nation There Is a Messenger, So When Their Messenger Comes The Matter Is Decided Between Them With Justice And They Are Not Wronged."

- May The Peace And Mercy Of Allah Forever Be Upon Him

Table of Contents

ACKNOWLEDGMENTS

Malachi Chapter 4 Verse 5:

Behold, I Will Send You Elijah the Prophet Before The Coming Of The Great And Dreadful Day Of The Lord

In The Name of Allah, The Beneficent, The Most Merciful. All Praise Is Due to Our Father, The Most Hon. Mr. Elijah Muhammad. We Forever Thank Allah For Raising from Among Us Our Saviour Master Fard Muhammad, And We Thank Allah for Muhammad, His Perfect Slave.

The Hon. Mr. Elijah Muhammad Is the Father of Us All. He Taught Us to Be Muslims. He Turned the Hearts of Our People Back To Our Roots. He Taught That the Blackman Is the Original Man, The Maker, Owner, and God Of The Planet Earth. He Made Us X Negroes, X Slaves, and X Christians. He Raised Us Out of The Mental Graves of Ignorance and Into the Ever-Living Light That The Blackman Is God, And The White Man Is The Devil.

Our Father's Mission Was to Prepare Us for The Arrival Of The Saviour, Whom He Would Raise, Commission, Make Holy And Teach To Establish The New World Kingdom Of Islam.

This Is the Judgment Day. You Are Judged by Your Acceptance Of The Teachings Of The Honorable Mr. Elijah Muhammad. You Will Not Be Accepted If You Do Not Believe In Elijah. You Cannot Accept Fard Unless You Believe in Our Father First.

The Saviour Is Now Among Us Doing His Work of Gathering His People. He Will Lead Us Eastward to Reclaim Our Own Land and Nation Under The Banner Of The Sun, Moon, And Star, Which Is Our Holy And Universal Flag Of Islam

HOLY QUR'AN CHAPTER 47 SECTION 1 VERSE 2:

"And those who believe and do good and believe in that which has been revealed to Muhammad and it is the truth from their lord, he will remove their evil from them and improve their condition."

May Allah forever bless our Father . . . Elijah.

> "Though I might seem insignificant to you,
> nevertheless, I am the man."
> The Honorable Elijah Muhammad

> "I am Elijah, the man prophesied of in the Bible.
> The Bible teaches you that He must first come,
> meaning He must first come before God to make
> a way for God to Come."
>
> (The Theology of Time, page 323)
>
> The Honorable Elijah Muhammad
>
> The Honorable Elijah Muhammad

ALI'S PRAYER

I bear witness that there is no God, besides Allah and Muhammad is His Soul.

O' Allah protect me against weakness and turn away from me the lustfulness of men.
None can grant strength and power but Thee.

O' Allah please answer my prayers, forgive me my sins, bestow upon me the highest intentions and a long life to do Thy will.

O' Allah make me to stand firm in righteousness for surely I am Thy slave. I have no help   besides Thee. I am Thy slave.

Show me Thy signs of wisdom and understanding, for surely I am Thy slave.

Amen

THE MUSLIM RESIGNATION

IN THE NAME OF ALLAH IN MUHAMMAD, THE BENEFICENT THE MERCIFUL

I come from Allah, Allah is my goal, therefore no trial or misfortune can upset my course in life, my peace, for my life has a much higher goal than just comfort alone. So come what may the contentment of my mind is never disturbed. PEACE! PEACE!

DECLARATION

In the Name of Allah and Muhammad

Though we walk through death's valley we have no fear nor do we grieve. We are persecuted and thrown into prisons for no reason but that we worship Allah in the person of Elijah Muhammad.

Our Allah has not forsaken us. We are cast down but we are not destroyed. We rely on Allah and it is to Him alone do we seek for help. Every prophecy has a turn so we are patient.

Celebrate the Father first and our Father will cause celebration to fall upon us like a nourishing rain. Teach the true identity of our Father, Elijah Muhammad, (my God who is worthy of praise and is praised much).

Regardless to whom or what our GOD, has declared that this is our day. The Judgment, Resurrection, Armageddon and the end of the devil's time is now.

Peace! Peace!
Ali Mahdi Muhammad
(Allah In Muhammad Speaks-July 17, 1990)

IN THE NAME OF ALLAH, THE BENEFICENT, THE MERCIFUL

DAYS OF THE SON OF MAN:
CONFUSION OF NATIONS

The prophecy of the coming of the Son of Man and the days of the Son of Man is almost the whole of the Bible, scriptures, histories and prophecies. The people who read the Bible should understand these things. You should want to read and understand.

Let us see what and who is the Son of Man who is mentioned here. We are all sons of some man, but this specifies the Son of Man coming in the Last Days to Judge man.

True understanding and the answers to these questions destroy any mistaken ideas or misunderstandings and prophecies of the Bible and Holy Qur'an concerning the coming of the Son of Man.

The true knowledge of Who is the Son of Man and Why He is Called the Son of Man destroys the teachings of the Christians concerning the prophecies of the Son of Man and the coming of the Son of Man. This forces understanding upon the world that is blind to the knowledge of Who and Why He is Called the Son of Man . . . especially the once slave of the white slave-masters.

The white Christians have never taught the true theology of scriptures to their Black Slave; therefore they do not know Who to look for. They look for something other than a man to usher in the Judgment and Judge the world according to its sins.

The Son of Man is the Son of a Man. He is not a spirit as the ignorant are prone to believe. He is the Son of Original Man, the Black Man.

The Bible does not teach you that He is the son of mankind. Mankind is the made-man, the white man. The Great Mahdi is the Son of the Original Man, the Black Man.

The Son of mankind is the made man, the white man whom the Original Man, the Black Man, drove out of the Garden of Eden.

The Son of Man, spoken of as Coming in the Last Days, is the Son of Original Man. Therefore they have it right when they say He is the Son of Man . . . that is the Original Man, the Black Man.

The Great Mahdi, the God and Judge Who is now Present in the World, Master Fard Muhammad To Whom Praises are Due forever, taught me that His Father was a real Black Man. His Father went up into the mountains (governments of the Caucasians) picking out a white woman to marry so that she would give birth to a son looking white but yet the Father is Black.

This makes the preachings of the Christians that He is a Made Man to take the burden of seeking the Lost-Found people from out of the midst of their captors who are white. He would do this work in a Day that they least expected. Therefore the Bible says he Came without observation as a thief in the night (night of Spiritual darkness) Bible 1 Th 5:2.

11

As to the days of the Son of Man, I would rather say they refer to years rather than days consisting of twenty-four (24) hours.

The Holy Qur'an also refers to it as the "Days" of Allah. This means "years" as it takes years to remove a whole world and bring in a new one. There is so much that has to be done. People have to be convinced that He is Justified to remove the world of sin, for the world of sin has ruled the people for 6,000 years. There are so many people who are sold to the idea of wicked world rulers.

The Days of the Son of Man represent the Days (Years) that He will Be Judging the world and gathering, teaching, and training His People right in the midst of this wicked world. His people have gotten experience of the wicked work and its teachings and yet live in the midst of it. Their living in the midst of the evil world and yet avoiding it proves their worthiness since they have gotten experience living in the evil world and now they turn to righteousness while they are still in the midst of the evil world. These people have an experience of both evil and good. Then if these are brought out of the evil world, these people are the people that he said he Saved out of the Fire. The Holy Qur'an says that we were on a Brink of Fire.

The Son of Man . . . the Bible is specific in its prophecy concerning this man. It tells us that we should make no mistake for there is no other prophecy of anything other than a Man coming and judging us. We all have been preaching of the day of the Son of Man. The mistaken idea that God is a spook or spirit is due to that which was added by you and your enemy while all the time He is telling you that He is The Son of Man.

The Great Mahdi, the Saviour of His People . . . Bible Mt. 1:21 prophesied that He Was Born to Save His People from sin. They were guilty of the same sin as that of their evil teacher, for they practiced the same sin.

Upon the coming of God, the Son of Man, He being the Just Judge of Man and man-kind, He forgave us our sins because we are not guilty of that which we did not know.

The man-kind (white man) taught us from the cradle to follow after them. They separated us from our Original People of Asia and Africa in order to do a thorough job of making us other than ourselves, the Original Black Man.

The white man went in and out of our grandparents until our blood became part of theirs . . . so we are today. This ties us up in his blood so that it will be easy for us to practice his way of life. In order to take us out of the life and doing of the mankind people, we had to have a knowledge of them.

It is the Great Mahdi, the Great Messiah, who is so prophesied of by the Christians. Yet the Pope of Rome and his priests are trying their utmost to deceive us concerning this Great Visit of God in Person. They try to deceive us into believing that this is not yet the Day of the Son of Man. They want you to believe that they still hold the reigns on the guidance for the Black People.

This defiant act is against the manifestation of the truth of them. By the Son of Man is the reason He is punishing them. He is putting priest against priest, church against church, and Christians against the Pope of Rome as we see it today Gen. 3:15. The Bible prophesies that the serpent will bruise the heel (followers) of the woman (Messenger). This means they would deceive the followers of the Messenger. But the Messenger will bruise the head of the serpent meaning the foundation of the chief of Christianity's way of teaching.

In the Days of the Son of Man there will be much trouble and confusion of Nations. Bible Is. 2.24:1 says the whole earth will be turned upside down and nations scattered abroad. The Bible says (Mt. 25:32) "Before Him shall be gathered all nations." The Holy Qur'an says, "You shall see all nations kneeling before Him and they shall be judged out of their own books." The government keeps a record of how they have ruled the people. They have a record of how they have judged the people.

The Holy Qur'an says that God will Judge them out of their own books which have the condemnation of their own evil and unjust judgment which they did give out to the people, especially the poor Black slave.

Boom, that is the end when this is accomplished. When the Son of Man proves that He is Justified in destroying the wicked, then they will be destroyed in the twinkling of an eye.

-by The Most Honorable Mr. Elijah Muhammad

(Reprint From N.W.K.O.I. Muhammad Speaks-1986)

**IN THE NAME OF ALLAH, THE BENEFICENT, THE MERCIFUL
AS-SALAAM ALAIKUM**

PRAYER IN ISLAM

"Surely prayer keeps (one) away from indecency and
evil; and certainly
the remembrance of Allah is the greatest (force) and
Allah
Knows what you do." (Holy Qur'an 29:45)

Surely the best way to strive to be upright in a sinful
world is to pray continuously to the One True God, whose
proper name is Allah, for guidance.

As we are generally sinful and easily yield to
temptation, it is only fitting to keep up prayer.

Allah, the One True God, has blessed us with the
universe. A sun to shine and brighten up the heavens, giving
light for us to see; warmth enabling us to live, and causing
vegetation to grow and all life to exist. We reside on the
planet through His will, so why should we not pray and
continuously thank him for this privilege?

He it is who created the atmosphere for us to breathe.
He it is who created all good vegetation for us to eat, plus
the fowl and other animals which we partake of daily. He it
is who created the beautiful atmosphere in which we live,
and which we, with our own hands, mutilate and destroy for
lack of proper guidance.

We cannot improve upon the nature in which Allah
(God) has created all beautiful things, yet we try. We cannot
substitute the original beauty with artificial creations, yet we

15

try. So let us realize the power of Allah, that without Him we cannot exist, and make obeisance to Allah through our prayers to Him.

Prayer is obligatory in Islam (the true religion). "And remember Allah's favor upon you and the covenant which He made with you, when you said, "We hear and we obey," and fear Allah. Surely Allah knows well what is in our minds.

"O ye who believe! Be steadfast in the cause of Allah, bearing witness in equity; and let not a people's enmity incite you to act otherwise than with justice," says the Holy Qur'an. Be always just; that is nearer righteousness. And fear Allah. Surely Allah is aware of what you do.

Allah has promised those who believe and do good deeds that they shall have forgiveness and a great reward (Holy Qur'an 8:10).

We owe our very lives to Allah, the Lord of all the worlds. Why should we not thank Him? Our every good thought we owe to Allah, the beneficent, the merciful. Surely as often as we sin, we turn to Him in prayer. He is most merciful and grants us pardon and oftentimes we drift back again to some other flaw. For this we must turn to Him again, asking to be forgiven. Surely Allah knows what is in our hearts, and what is more, he is oft-forgiving.

He it is who is the All Perfect One, who knows our imperfection and pardons most through His messenger. Remember: And the best way for remembrance of Allah (God) is through prayer.

The five prayers of the day are spiritual refreshments and he who cleanses himself in and out leaves no filthiness.

It would be an insult to invite His lord's holy spirit into a house the outside of which was filthy.

Why should we not pray five times a day to our Maker since we feed our bodies three times a day? What is so important that would keep us away from prayer to the Originator of the heavens and the earth?

Let us give praises to our God and submit ourselves to the Lord of the worlds and learn how to pray the right prayers in the right manner. Let us serve the One True God, whose proper name is Allah, in the right state.

"My Lord, make me to keep up prayer, and my offspring too. Our Lord, accept the prayer. Our Lord, grant Thy protection to me and to my parents and to the faithful on the day when the reckoning will be taken." (The prayer of the Muslims will get you an answer!)

Wa-Alaikum Salaam
Elijah Muhammad

(Reprint From Allah In Muhammad Speaks-December 17, 1987)

In The Name Of Allah, The Beneficent, The Most Merciful Saviour, Master Of The Day Of Requital To Him Alone Do I Submit And Seek Refuge

"MINISTER"

Dear Brother Minister:

The quality of being prepared is a necessary qualification of being a Minister. The best way to help me is by the methods I select for you. If you are not going to help the way I want you to help, it is best that you do not do anything. I'll do it myself. If I interpret scripture for you, tell those interpretations as I stated them. Tell your audience I told you. The people know you did not get it from yourself.

You are to follow the way I tell you to go. God gives it to me. I got the Message from Allah. I have nothing to do with the Message of Allah but deliver it to you. It is written that out of the Lamb's mouth came a two-edge sword (the truth) which was sufficient to destroy the lies of the beast. You should study the life and works of the Messengers in the Bible and Holy Qur'an. There is nothing in the Messenger's life which is not written in a book.

Study everything in the book. Defend the Messenger with everything you learn from the books pertaining to him and put it in the proper place and time. Study the Bible and Qur'an. You cannot take Yakub's history and defend it as I can. It is best that you teach the people what you heard me teach. You are bearing witness to the people that I am the man from God. You are to show proof that compares with predictions. You have not seen God but you believe that I have seen Him. You are teaching this to the people. This way you will make progress. Do not make the mistake of not keeping the Messenger in Front.

It is very tempting for you to make people think you got something from yourself. Allah is watching you. He is the one who exalts you. You must first learn if the people are believers. This is one of the main things holding Temples back. Beware of this Ministers, you must be tried. Maybe some of you may be put in jail and beaten but Allah will deliver you out of it all if you are true believers, as He did me and others. Hold on to what I have taught you about me and our work.

As Ministers, I want to assure you that you have no right to fear! I am not responsible for belief. Allah holds me responsible for the clear deliverance of the Message. Allah told me, "Nobody wants us but me." This we know to be true. Allah blesses us with safety. As Allah told me and the Holy Qur'an teaches the Messenger, "All fear shall be removed from you and nor shall you grieve." Do I show any fear of anything to you? I rely on Allah.

Do like I tell you and you will be successful. If you have the least doubt in me and the Messenger of Allah, do not follow me. I am Warning you. If I find any Minister acting weak, out he goes. If you have any weakness, it will. Forget about your wants. The Holy Qur'an teaches do it like the last Messenger says. Allah's greatest desire and my greatest desire is for you to believe the truth. The Holy Qur'an is a Message put in the mouth of the Messenger. We are building a New World. I have to follow close to my Lord. You have to follow close to me to follow Him.

The Holy Qur'an says: Whatever Allah and His Apostle say, you say, we hear and obey.

If Allah allows or Causes me to be killed or Die a Natural Death that does not mean that you should turn back or take what I have taught to be false.

I am the last Messenger to you. The ones coming after me are Messengers, of those who do not. It was Noah's God who talked to him about the flood. It was Moses whom God talked to about the destruction of Pharaoh.

Do the best you can and your names will be like stars.

May the peace and blessings of Allah forever be upon you.

As-Salaam-Alaikum
Your Brother,
Elijah Muhammad
Messenger of Allah

(Reprint From: Allah In Muhammad Speaks-December 17, 1987)

MASTER FARD MUHAMMAD

In The Name of Allah Who Come in The Person of
Master Fard Muhammad in The Year 1930. W shall
praise is name for 1,000 years.

Peace. Peace.

ALI MAHDI MUHAMMAD

The Leader and Teacher Of
The New World Nation of Islam

1. Ali Mahdi Muhammad is the Spiritual Guide and Leader and Teacher of the New World Nation of Islam.

2. Ali Mahdi Muhammad was born in Winter Haven, Florida, March 31, 1939. He moved to Newark, New Jersey in the early 1940's. He was raised in the streets of Newark's 2nd and 3rd wards. And he converted to the teachings of the Honorable Mr. Elijah Muhammad in the 1950's. He is one of the original 13 Muslims in the city of Newark, and helped establish Newark Mosque number 25.

3. On February 26, 1960, at the annual Savior's Day Convention in Chicago, Illinois, Ali Mahdi Muhammad was commissioned Field Supreme Captain by the Honorable Mr. Elijah Muhammad, along with Fard Saviour who was commissioned National Field Supreme Minister.

4. In 1960 The Honorable Mr. Elijah Muhammad ordered Ali Mahdi Muhammad and Fard Saviour to establish the first Academy of Islam. They fulfilled that mission at Trenton State Prison from 1960 to 1965.

5. In 1965-1966 Ali Mahdi Muhammad and Fard Saviour returned to Mosque number 25 and experienced rejection by the officials there, notwithstanding their ranks of National Field Supreme Minister and Field Supreme Captain. Moreover, their belief that the Honorable Elijah Muhammad was Allah

in Person was scorned and ridiculed in fulfillment of such prophecies as the Jews who rejected Jesus.

6. As a result of the rejection by the Old World officials, Ali Mahdi Muhammad saw the handwriting on the wall and the fulfillment of Mr. Elijah Muhammad's teachings that the Nation of Islam was honey combed with hypocrites and disbelievers. That the Old World of Islam was going out, and that a New World of Islam was coming in. And the New World of Islam was established in 1966 fulfilling such histories as the Deportation of the Moon.

7. Ali Mahdi Muhammad is the only minister of the Honorable Elijah Muhammad who did not leave his post when Elijah Muhammad passed the title of Allah on. Simply put, Ali Mahdi Muhammad upheld and taught Elijah when Imam Warith Deen Muhammad took the nation into Sunni Islam.

8. Our Father commissioned Bro. Fard to build the House of our Father's desire (New World) and after teaching us for 15 years he left. Master Fard Saviour commissioned General Muhammad and after 26 years he left Brother Ali to complete that work.

9. Ali Mahdi Muhammad is the author of several books, including Uncle Yah Yah and The Al Fard.

(Reprint From: Allah In Muhammad Speaks-Oct/Nov. 1995)

IN THE NAME OF ALLAH IN MUHAMMAD

PEACE! PEACE!

RESURRECTION

In the beginning, God created the heavens and the earth. Of course, we know that the Almighty Black God of the universe has no beginning or end, so we are exploring the start of a new cycle of our endless history.

There was no heaven and no earth until our Father, The Most Hon. Mr. Elijah Muhammad, created this SPACE for us to exist in. This is our universe, this is our only reality. Outside of the teachings of our Father, we have nothing.

The first stage of the resurrection is the creation of Adam and Eve, (the creation of Ali Mahdi and His family, also known as the Divine Staff of Allah God). It is these few that Elijah, (my God) raised first. They are the first people, Gods and Goddesses of a New World of Islam.

The gathering and raising of the Divine family as the Staff of God is the most important work of Elijah, (my God) because it is these few who will initiate the change of worlds and resurrect the masses of our poor, deaf, dumb and blind Holy Tribe of Shabazz, the so-called American Negro.

Allah will stop at nothing to bring this change of worlds about. He uses any and everything in the universe to help Him create this Divine family of Gods. This first family is the most blessed of Allah, God. Even the children of these shall see visions and predict the future in their dreams.

No power is great enough to stop this change of worlds and the resurrection of God's people.

24

Ali Mahdi Muhammad and His family, the Divine Staff of God are lost in the light of which they are created. That is why they were called the children of the Light of God in the Holy Qur'an and Bible.

This means that they can't and don't want to see outside of the knowledge, wisdom and understanding given to us by Our Father the Hon. Mr. Elijah Muhammad, the last God of the Old World and the first God of the New World Nation of Islam.

The Great Mahdi is now reclaiming His own. He reaches within Himself and the black earth to find His people. He, then teaches and trains them in the science of the New World, not the old world which is on its way out. This New World will not accept anything of the old world of slavery, suffering and death.

Don't try to judge Muhammad with your evil minds of this world. You will find yourself fighting against the very God you say you serve.

The Hon. Mr. Elijah Muhammad has created the Sun, Moon and Stars of the New Universe. He has given us our place in the Sun. We are proud to be Elijah Muslims and Citizens of His New World Nation of Islam.

Wake-up Blackman, this is Your Day.

Peace! Peace!
Ali Mahdi Muhammad
(Reprint From: Allah In Muhammad Speaks-Mar/Apr 1988)

**IN THE NAME OF ALLAH
THE BENEFICIENT, THE MERCIFUL**

PEACE! PEACE!

The Hearts Of The Children Turning Back To Our Father, The Honorable Elijah Muhammad

<u>Allah, is the God, of everything. But you and I would have no idea that Allah is God if it was not for the teachings of our Father the Most Hon. Mr. Elijah Muhammad.</u>

The blackman of America was deaf, dumb and blind until he heard the life giving message of Elijah Muhammad. Many of us rose up to great heights and was considered wise.

But the time of darkness had not run its course and the nation was to sleep until the worlds of satan was finished. It was a deep sleep and only a few of the scientist of Islam remained awake.

The Nation of Islam and the teachings of our Father was not dead, but in a deep sleep. That sleep was for a divine purpose; just as the wheat seed sleeps in the winter then springs to life in the spring, so it is with the teachings of our Father, the Most Honorable Mr. Elijah Muhammad.

We have been like the prodigal son. We know our Father's teachings are divine, but that God's scripture be fulfilled we had to go into the wilderness and lay dead until it is time to return to our Father's house and teachings.

I am your brother and I am calling you to stand up, clean-up and take your post in the House of our Father's desire. The New World Nation of Islam.

You must now return to the God consciousness and join hands with me. We are now in our time. The Banner of our Father, the Sun, Moon and Star must now be uplifted for now and forever.

The New World Nation of Islam is now coming into existence, it is built on the foundation of the teachings of our Father, the last God, of the Old World and the first God, of the New World.

All you Ministers, Captains, Lieutenants, and Secretaries whose hearts and minds still germinate the truth of Elijah, must come forth now and join me in raising our poor black brothers and sisters.

May Allah in the person of Master Fard, the Great Mahdi, bless us to wake up, clean-up and take our post in our Father's house the New World Nation of Islam.

Peace . . . Peace . . .
Ali Mahdi Muhammad

(Reprint From: Allah in Muhammad Speaks Mar/Apr 1988)

IN THE NAME OF ALLAH IN MUHAMMAD

THE TRUTH

We are living in the Transformation. This is the time when we grow out of our human sense and worldly understanding into our God sense and universal understanding.

The Holy Month of Ramadan, is the one time of year that we (New World Muslims) turn off from all worldly vanities and keep to the remembrance of Allah. At this time we, Muslims, must let Allah's will be done. 100% concentration on prayer and fasting, transforms us from the low material world to the high spiritual world of God; also from ordinary to the extraordinary. We are what we practice.

During this Holy Month of praying and fasting all New World Muslims are taught to fight the wicked devil and cleanse ourselves of evil habits such as: hatred, pride, ego tripping, anger, jealousy, lust, possessiveness, indifference, fighting and killing each other. All the above evil habits are poisonous.

During this Ramadan, we Muslims must practice the will of Allah, which is love, peace, happiness, wanting for your brother what you want for yourself, keeping your word, not lying, service to Allah, thinking 10 times before you act and sharing with the believers what Allah, has blessed you with. We also, remember constantly that prayer is the greatest force against evil and the source of everything. Prayer takes you directly to Allah's kingdom within the heart of all Muslims.

Pray: "Let Muhammad forever be blessed."

Our Father, the Most Hon. Mr. Elijah Muhammad, Last God of the Old world and First God of the New World, taught us that, There's no spirit without a man and no man without a spirit. He taught us that there is no more mystery gods that we can't see until after you die in the sweet bye and bye. God, is a man and have always manifested himself in a man. Such a man is now among you today in the person of Master Fard Muhammad, the Great Mahdi.

So let us remember this Ramadan: The more we concentrate on keeping the peace and the attributes of Allah in our mind, we now transform as an angel (agent) of the New World Nation, created by our Father Allah to lead the world in Righteousness.

Make this our best Ramadan. May Allah, bless us all.
Peace! Peace!
Ali Mahdi Muhammad

(Reprint From: Allah In Muhammad Speaks-December 17, 1987)

Dec. 20, 1968

IN THE NAME OF ALLAH IN MUHAMMAD

DIVINE UNITY

Written by: Bro. Field Supreme Captain Muhammad Ali

Almighty Allah, God, is in Person among us, here in the wilderness of North America, today. But do not ask the Holy Prophet to arrange an audience for you to meet with Almighty God, Allah. It is not vouch-safe that Allah should meet and speak with us. Allah is aware of each and every one of us. He knows all of our problems. This is why He raised from among us His last and greatest prophet, Master Fard Muhammad, and gave Him perfect and unequaled guidance to give us, so let our Prophet continue to meet with Allah and let him inform us of Almighty God, Allah's will and Divine Revelation. This is better for us, so that we do not cause trouble for the Holy Prophet, and do harm to ourselves. None can come into the presence of Allah except whom He pleases.

A believer may visit or meet with the Holy Prophet for consultation but he must let Headquarters or those in authority arrange his audience for him. You should always give the Holy Prophet a gift when you meet with Him. It is good that you do so in the eyes of Allah, but if you cannot afford a gift, then say: "Praise be to Allah, the Lord of the Mighty Throne of Power, and Muhammad is His Last and Greatest Prophet, Allah is the Most Merciful." When you meet with the Holy Prophet, be as humble and respectful as you can be. Do not be forward in the presence of the Prophet

and do not raise your voice above the Prophet's voice. Do not call out or speak to him as we speak to each other. Give the Prophet your gift, take care of your business and leave. Do not hang around the home of the prophet idly.

Read Qur'an Ch. 33, section 7, verse 53. It says: "O you who believe, enter not the house of The Prophet unless permission is given to you for a meal, not waiting while cooking is being finished, but when you are invited, enter, and when you have taken food, disperse, not seeking to listen to talk. Surely this gives the Prophet trouble, but he forbears from you and Allah forbears not from the truth. And when you ask of them any goods, ask of them from behind a curtain. This is purer for your hearts and their hearts. And it behooves you not to give trouble to the Messenger of Allah, nor to marry His wives after Him ever. Surely this is evil in the sight of Allah."

Also verse 56 of the same chapter says: "Surely Allah and His angels bless the Prophet. O you who believe, call for blessings on him and salute him with a (becoming) salutation." So always give the Holy Prophet a gift if you can afford one. Those of you who are in authority among the companions of the Holy Prophet should not wait around the Prophet's house nor follow him about seeking to be the first to hear every new revelation that comes to him. If the

Prophet desires you to be in his company, let him send for you. Do not impose upon him because you are free to do so. Allah and His Prophet estimate a believers worth by the work that the believer does. Now surely the greatest work in the eyes of Allah and His Prophet is fighting in the way of Allah for the salvation and independence of our people and teaching Islam.

So, by all means get out into the land and do good work for Allah and the Prophet, this is better for you. The Saviour has never failed to give us the new revelations as they come to him, so no believer will be left without the proper guidance.

Teach Fard's Fruit to fight for the Independence of our people and to be brave, to fight with all their strength, to have courage and to fear no one besides Allah, and to never turn on your heels when fighting the enemy. Teach Fard's Fruit, the knowledge, wisdom and understanding that the Saviour has taught us. Teach Fard's Fruit, to be proud of themselves and to be an example of love, unity and brotherhood. Teach Fard's Fruit, to never fail to go to their brother's aid and to depend on each other for food, clothing and shelter. Teach them to protect the families and properties of each other. The Saviour has brought about Divine Unity among the 24 Islamic Scientists, now it is our duty to teach this doctrine of Unity to Fard's Fruit.

May Allah Bless You,
As-Salaam-Alaikum

IN THE NAME OF ALLAH IN MUHAMMAD

MUSLIMS MUST PRAY

He Allah, Is The One, True And Living God, To Whom We Muslims Submit To And Seek For Help. We Depend On Allah, And He Doesn't Need Us.

We, New World Muslims are as babies just born to our Father the Hon. Mr. Elijah Muhammad. As an infant nation we have little control of our actions, emotions, our hands, feet and body functions. But as we develop and grow, we learn that each and every body part have it's own ethnicity. Each part of the New World body, is created and ordained to function in accord with Allah's universal plan. You might not like a thing, but Allah, has ordained it.

The New World Nation of Islam, are the God-head tribe of Shabbazz. Also known as Elijah Muslims. Ali Mahdi Muhammad, is our leader and teacher and the spiritual son of Elijah Muhammad, the Last, God of the old world and the First God, of the New World of Islam.

Thanks, thanks, to Allah, the Beneficent and the Most Merciful. It is time to pray that the divine truth given to us by our Father, Hon. Mr. Elijah Muhammad, reach the hearts of every Muslim and cause a new age of true unity between Islamic Nations.

O' Allah, bless us Muslims to want for our brother what we want for ourselves. Our Lord, please stop the Muslims from killing fellow Muslims and protect us from treating each other wrong.

We pray that all Muslims believe in and dedicate themselves to following the divine guidance in the Holy Qur'an, and scripture of our prophets and great leaders of Islam. We pray Allah, bless us to keep the peace and to keep our word. Bless us O Allah, to offer a helping hand to our fellow Muslims whenever the need arises. Bless us to have no fear except of Allah. Bless us to teach Islam to all who seek the truth and let us fight in Allah's way that we may be among those drawn closet to Thee. May Allah, bless us all with a happy and a successful Ramadan.

Peace! Peace!

Your Brother, A.M. Muhammad

(Reprint From: Allah In Muhammad Speaks-December 17, 1987)

"The General"

IMPORTANT BULLETIN FOR ELIJAH MUSLIMS

In the name of Allah, The Beneficent, The Most Merciful. In the person of our Spiritual Father, The Most Hon. Mr. Elijah Muhammad, the Last God of The Old World and The First God of The New World Hereafter.

He is the First and the Last, the Beginning and the Ending. He was Dead but is Alive forever more. He has the Keys to Heaven and Hell. And we forever give praise to Master Fard Muhammad the Great Mahdi, who was to come and has come.

As Salaam Alaikum

All Believers in our Spiritual Father The Most Hon. Elijah Muhammad must return to the path that He prepared for us.

He said, "Hold fast to Allah in the person of Master Fard Muhammad the Great Mahdi and follow me. You, My Wonderful Followers are registered in the table of my memory to which I shall turn every day of my life."

As Salaam Alaikum
Your Brother,
Elijah Muhammad
Messenger of Allah

IN THE NAME OF ALLAH IN MUHAMMAD

My Beloved Brothers and Sisters,

I am your brother, General Ali Mahdi Muhammad. I am the Field Supreme Minister of the Old World Nation of Islam and the New World Nation of Islam who was to come and has come to restore us back to our own Holy Nation of Islam, as ordered by our spiritual Father, the Honorable Elijah Muhammad, and to destroy those who have destroyed us. All praises are forever due to our Father, Allah, in the person of the Honorable Elijah Muhammad.

Be not deceived. Nothing is wrong. It is all good. Didn't our Father teach us that our Kingdom can't come until there be a falling away first? The bible says in Revelations Chapter 12: The Dragon or the Chief Hypocrites will drag some of our Stars out of where our Father placed them. Most are now thrown down. Many of the believers have been deceived and, or cast down. But that is as it should be. The prophets don't lie.

It is said that before the coming of the dreadful day of the Lord, we must turn the hearts of the children back to our Father. Someone had to turn them (children) away if we must now turn them (children) back to our Father's teachings.

Nothing is wrong. It is all good and it is on time, all the time. Allah, in the person of the Son of Man (the original man, the Honorable Elijah Muhammad), Master Fard Muhammad, The Great Mahdi, is in control of all our affairs.

Everyone did not fall away. A few were ordered to hold their post until the men of sin (in the nation) were revealed. The chief hypocrites who would turn our Father's house into a den of thieves had to be made known.

We must acknowledge and honor those beautiful brothers and sisters who believed in our Father, the Honorable Elijah Muhammad, regardless to whom or what. Those who refused to let go and turn their backs after they accepted the teaching of our Father. Some of you saw that the enemy (the devils and hypocrites) was trying to change or destroy the Nation of Islam and our Father's teachings. Many of you left the Nation, but you did not leave your belief in The Honorable Elijah Muhammad. You saw that the only way for you to hold on was to leave and maintain your faith yourself.

You, my beloved black brothers and sisters, who held on, are the most blessed of the Honorable Elijah Muhammad's followers.

We, the Field Supreme Staff had no choice, but to hold on. We were ordered by our Father, "To be not deceived and to carry out our mission regardless to whom, or what." We the Field Staff could only hear and obey.

We the Field Supreme Staff salute you and welcome you into your own, The New World Nation of Islam.

This is the Dawn of our spiritual Day. We must now raise our people, the Blackman, so-called negro, X-slaves of America to be the greatest nation on this earth.

If you are ready to stand up and help build the House of Our Father's Desire, not changing one word of the Honorable Elijah Muhammad's teachings, then write to:

New World Nation of Islam
P.0. Box 8466
Newark, NJ 07108
 888-213-2409
 truth@newworldnationislam.com

May the peace and blessings of Allah forever be upon us all. Peace to you in this world and Peace to you in the New World Hereafter.

As-Salaam-Alaikum
Your Brother,
General A.M. Muhammad Field Supreme Minister

IN THE NAME OF ALLAH IN MUHAMMAD

STANDARD OPENING FOR MINISTERS AND STUDENT MINISTERS

In the Name of Allah, the Beneficent, the Most Merciful. All Praise is due to our Father, the Most Honorable Mr. Elijah Muhammad. We forever thank Allah, for raising from among us our Saviour Master Fard Muhammad, and we thank Allah for Muhammad, His Perfect Slave.

Peace! Peace!

The Honorable Mr. Elijah Muhammad is the Father of us all. He taught us to be Muslims. He turned the hearts of our people back to our roots. He taught that the Blackman is the original man, the maker, owner and God of the planet Earth. He made us X-Negroes, X-Slaves, and X-Christians. He raised us out of the mental graves of ignorance and into the ever living light that the Blackman is God, and the White man is the devil.

Our Father's mission was to prepare us for the arrival of the Saviour, Whom He would raise, commission, make Holy and teach to establish the New Kingdom of Islam.

This is the Judgment Day. You are judged by your acceptance of the teachings of the Honorable Mr. Elijah Muhammad. You cannot accept Fard unless you believe in our Father first.

The Saviour is now among us doing His work of gathering His people. He will lead us Eastward to reclaim our Own land and Nation under the Banner of the Sun, Moon and Star, which is our Holy and Universal Flag of Islam. Today you will be blessed to hear the teachings of our Saviour, Master Fard Muhammad, as taught by one of His Ministers who received this Divine word from Allah's Spokesman and National Representative, General Ali Mahdi Muhammad.

- End of Opening -

At this Point Introduce the Speaker.

Date Issued: Sept. 30, 1985
General Muhammad

As truth cannot be purchased, this book is a gift to you in exchange for your contribution.

The New World Nation Of Islam uses these books to help General Ali Mahdi Muhammad establish the house of our Father's desire.

"They ask you (O Muhammad) what they should spend
in charity. Say: Whatever you spend with a good heart, give it to parents, relatives, orphans, the helpless, and travelers in need. Whatever good you do, God is aware
of it."

The Holy Qur'an, 2:215

New World Nation of Islam Publications
PO Box 8466
Newark, NJ 07108
888-213-2409

The 1st Edition (2011) Compiled, Arranged, Layout by: MGT/Sisters, Hafida Zakat Ali | Muqarabun Ali | M.W. Ali

BOOK 2:
DIVINE WISDOM OF A. M. MUHAMMAD

OPENING:

IN THE NAME OF ALLAH IN MUHAMMAD

I will raise them up a Prophet from among their brethren, like unto thee <u>and will put my words in his mouth; and he shall speak unto them all that I shall command him.</u>

And it shall come to pass, that whoever will not harken unto my words <u>which he shall speak in my name</u>, I will require it of him.

Deuteronomy, CHAPTER 18, VERSES 18-19

All Praises due to Allah in Muhammad. It gives us a great but humble pleasure to be blessed with this opportunity to make a joyous noise unto our Lord. The 'Great Mahdi' Brother Ali Mahdi Muhammad. The Leader of the New World Nation of Islam.

For surely our Lord (Bro. A.M. Muhammad) has clearly manifested himself as the last Minister and Standard Bearer of the Divine teachings of the Hon. Mr. Elijah Muhammad.

He (Bro. A.M. Muhammad) and he alone has truly fulfilled the above Bible scripture from the book of <u>Deuteronomy</u>, as it relates to the last Minister (Bro. A.M. Muhammad) receiving instructions from his Lord, The Hon.

44

Mr. Elijah Muhammad. Quote: "And he shall speak unto them all that I shall command him."

Bro. A.M. Muhammad is and always has been a true echo of the Voice of One Crying (Elijah) in the wilderness of North America. He (A.M. Muhammad) has dedicated his total being and life to the fulfillment of building the House of our Father's Desire, The New World Nation of Islam and leading our people the (so-called Negro) away from the murderous oppression of the wicked white blue-eyed Devils.

We thank Allah for our Lord Bro. A.M. Muhammad and the Spiritual Resurrection of all those who believe, accept and follow the Divine teachings of our Father, the Hon. Mr. Elijah Muhammad . . . Allah is God.

PEACE! PEACE!

In The Name of Our Father The Most Honorable Mr. Elijah Muhammad to Whom All Of The Praise Is Due. And We Thank Allah In The Person Of Master Fard Muhammad For His Perfect Slave Muhammad. We, The True Believers Of Allah And This Day Of Judgement In Which We Ow Live, Greet You In Our New World Nation Of Islam's Greetings Of Peace To You In The Old World And Peace To You In The New World Hereafter... Peace, Peace.

DIVINE WISDOM OF BROTHER A.M. MUHAMMAD!

In the Name of Allah in Muhammad and the True Believers of Almighty God Allah!

The following articles that we have been blessed to gather and place in this booklet, come from an accumulation of columns delivered to us (the Believers) by our Lord Brother Ali 'Mahdi' Muhammad. We pray to Allah in Muhammad that all of you who read these columns be blessed with divine perception and a Clear insight. For these truths will certainly set you free.

PEACE, PEACE!

Open Letters To The Believers!

David and Solomon: And the Lord said unto his Lord, "Sit on my right hand while I make your enemies your foot stool."

Jesus says, "All Praises are due to our Father." The Most Honorable Mr. Elijah Muhammad is the Father of the Jesus of today. Elijah said His Lord is Allah in the Person of Master Fard Muhammad. Jesus the Christ.

Moses says his Lord is Jehovah and Aaron says his Lord is Moses.

There is no confusion here for those who accept all the prophets. We know that all the prophets of Allah brought the truth. They taught that He, Allah is one God and the Prophets agree that in the day of judgment, God Himself would be present among us. That we would know and recognize him as we know the faces of our children.

This day with God in the person of Master Fard Muhammad in our midst makes our Islamic wisdom complete and perfect.

Let the Believers rejoice. Let the Believers teach Islam. This is a New Day, this is our day and all of the truth of God and the devil must be made manifest.

All we have to do is follow our Father's program under the guidance of our Leader and Prophet Master Fard Muhammad. He is our Divinely appointed guide of the New World Nation of Islam.

IN THE NAME OF ALLAH IN MUHAMMAD

Our Saviour, Allah, ordained Muhammad, the Rock with 12 Springs flowing from it. He, Muhammad will teach His people and lead them eastward, with books written by the divine fingers of Allah in the Person of our Father and New books written by our Brother Muhammad.

Separation is a Must!

We are those angels who are in hell but are not destroyed by hell. We are in the world but not of it. We are not attached to anything but Allah and Muhammad.

Gods succeed one another. When it's time for a change Allah raises one to bring about that change. Just as Allah raised Muhammad to be the Master of the way to the New World, so Muhammad has raised you to be worthy of praise and praised and followed wherever you go. Muhammad is one with Allah and, you are one with Muhammad.

Our people now seek enlightenment. Get as much knowledge as you can. Never stop studying the divine lessons of our Father. Get ready to teach hundreds and thousands. You must read and grow strong in our knowledge, the Supreme Wisdom.

Holy Qur'an Chapter 23 verse 27, 28 and 29:

"And say my Lord cause me to land a blessed landing and thou are the best of those who bring to land."

As it was in the days of Noah, so it is today. Read Chapter 3 Section 7; also Chapter 3 Section 18 Verse 178:

"Allah will not leave the believer in the condition in which you are until he <u>separates the evil from the good</u>."

Now that the foundation of our Father's House (the staff) is complete the rest of the work will be much easier with the help and protection of Allah. Let us start our work on this New Day with the Song of Victory and the knowledge of our sure success.

"The day when the spirit and the Angels stand in rank none shall speak except he whom the Beneficent permits and he speaks aright. That is the true day so whoever desires may take refuge with his Lord." - Holy Qur'an Chapter 78 verse 38-39.

May Allah continue to bless us all.

Your Brother, Muhammad . . . Spokesman for Allah

PS: We have the highest Islam known. Hold fast to our Father's teachings and watch how quick we enter heaven. Remember we are Shabazz, the God Tribe.

(Reprint From ALLAH IN MUHAMMAD SPEAKS . . . Volume 1-4 April 17, 1987

HEREAFTER WHAT?

We have the help and protection of Allah. Any attack on us is an attack against Almighty God Allah himself.

Those who know the teaching of our Father to be the divine truth will love us and help us in every way. The wise can see and know that we are the children of the life-giving light of our Father. Our actions make them bear witness that we are the best Muslims.

The devils cast out a flood of propaganda (dirty water), but like it was in the days of Noah, as soon as the dirty water drowns, destroys and passes away God establishes an all new civilization.

HEREAFTER THE FLOOD

That day you will see the Great Mahdi and his staff of Holy Angels standing in rank. Holy Qur'an 78: 38-39.

In the name of Allah in the Person of our Father the Most Honorable Mr. Elijah Muhammad. We forever thank him for raising from among us the Great Mahdi, the Crusher of the wicked.

Bible reference. Revelations 19: 11-21

"O you who believe fight those of the disbelievers who are near to you and let them find firmness in you. And know that Allah is with those who keep their duty." Holy Qur'an 9: 123

<u>HEREAFTER THE FLOOD</u>

It is because of our dedication to our beloved Father the Most Honorable Mr. Elijah Muhammad that the devil seeks to destroy us.

No. We the true believers do not turn our backs on our Father's teachings. We are not afraid of your threats. The threats of the devil cannot hurt the true believers. God, Allah is our protection.

Let it be known that we will prosper, even though the disbelievers, hypocrites and paid informers are doing their best to help the devil stop us.

> "Surely Allah has bought from the believers their persons and their property- theirs (in return) is the garden. They fight in Allah's way, so they slay and are slain. It is a promise which is binding on him in the Torah and the Gospel and the Qur'an. And who is more faithful to his promise than Allah? Rejoice therefore in your bargain which you have made. That is the mighty Achievement." Holy Qur'an 9:111

<u>HEREAFTER THE FLOOD!</u>

The three Greatest words in the Universe are 'Allah is God'. Please read the Bible Psalms 2: 1-12 and the Holy Qur'an 48: 1-10

May Allah forever bless us all.

Peace, Peace And Love . . .
Your Brother, Muhammad

(Reprint From: ALLAH IN MUHAMMAD SPEAKS . . . VOLUME 1-18 . . . 11/17/88)

DIFFERENT MUSLIMS
By ALI MAHDI MUHAMMAD

They continue daily to accuse us of having our own kind of Islam. We say of course we do; as the Chinese do, as the Russian Muslims do, as the North Muslims from the East, or West Muslims. The New World Nation of Islam, whose founder is none other than the Hon. Elijah Muhammad, you know him as the Messenger of Allah, had the Islam created for us. You have your way. We have ours.

Don't be foolish and judge us before you see our works. See if what we, New World Muslims do. Then you can judge if what we do is right.

Every follower of the Honorable Mr. Elijah Muhammad must teach what Elijah taught him. We are responsible for teaching the Islam taught us by Elijah, our Father in faith, the Last God, of the Old World. And the First God of the New World. Wherever you are brothers and sisters, teach. Teach in the open or teach from behind the closed door, just don't forget your responsibility to teach.

Allah, created Peace. Also, he created all the different ways to get to the time in life that you can say, "I submit entirely to the will of Allah." He allows no false ways. He nourishes only the true ways.

We, New World Muslims, follow the way of Elijah Muhammad. That is the way of the times. This Day-Right Now.

Only God, can prescribe a way for the Blackman of America to attain perfect Peace. And we are of those many different kinds of Muslims who submit to the will of Allah. Take it or leave it alone, or you may find yourself trying to oppose God.

PEACE, PEACE . . . Your Brother, Muhammad

(Reprint From ALLAH IN MUHAMMAD SPEAKS . . . VOLUME 1-8 . . . 7/17/87)

WE ARE ELIJAH MUSLIMS

I AM THAT I AM, THE FIRST AND THE LAST, THE ALPHA AND THE OMEGA
I AM HE WHO WAS DEAD AND IS ALIVE FOREVER MORE!!!

The above statement is profound. Our Father the Most Honorable Mr. Elijah Muhammad said that is the description of himself and in another sense, it referred to General Muhammad, the Crusher of the wicked, The Great Mahdi.

He Elijah is the first to recognize that Allah was a Man in the Person of Master Fard Muhammad and Elijah was the last to uphold our Saviour Master Fard.

Your Brother General Muhammad was the first to accept that Elijah is Allah God and he Muhammad is the last to uphold the teachings of our Father that Allah is a man in Person, Master Fard Muhammad the Great Mahdi.

If you Love my Father, you would love me. It's his work I am doing. ONLY ALLAH has charge of my life your life and the life of everything.

Learn this quote from Waldo Emerson, he said, "The simplest person who in his integrity worships God becomes God."

YOU SHOULD HELP TO BUILD THE HOUSE OF OUR FATHER'S DESIRE.

Never fight against people who Allah intends to bless. We, NEW WORLD NATION OF ISLAM MUSLIMS will not help the Satanic enemy in his fight against our Brother Muslim Nations and we Pray Allah you never Join our enemy (the White devil) to fight against us. We Pray Allah bless the unity of the Muslims.

THE NEW WORLD NATION OF ISLAM may seem insignificant to you now but the smallest seeds produce some of the tallest trees. WE ARE ELIJAH MUSLIMS AND PROUD OF IT. My God Allah has raised me and sent me and only mine will recognize me. Help us or leave Us alone!

All Praises are forever due to Allah the Lord of all the Worlds.

PEACE . . . PEACE . . . A.M. MUHAMMAD

(Reprint From ALLAH IN MUHAMMAD SPEAKS . . . VOLUME 1-13. . . 1/17/88)

IN THE NAME OF ALLAH IN MUHAMMAD . . .
PEACE, PEACE!

OUR FATHER

The Saviour taught me to always do the first things first!
Number one on our working list is to celebrate the Praise of
our Father, The Most Honorable Mr. Elijah Muhammad, the
last God of the old World and the first God of the New
World Nation of Islam. The work we are doing in raising the
Nation is our Father's work. He gave this duty to us. The
knowledge and wisdom all CAME FROM ELIJAH. Our
Father to whom we praise forever.

Elijah Muhammad, raised us from the mud of
civilization. He made us proud to be black. He made us stand
on our own black two feet. Allah in the person of Elijah
Muhammad, made us black men and women love discipline.
He taught us men and boys military training and to remain
loyal to our Father to the death and in the here and now, after
our Father (God in Person) passed the crown and the -
command on. We are ever loyal and serve all the days.

He Allah, taught our women and girls, all that they
would need to know about civilization. It is through the
Black and beautiful hands of our women (Queen Mother of
the planet earth) that a New Civilization is being fashioned.

Thanks, thanks to our Father Elijah Muhammad, Allah,
God, in Person.

Let the will of our Father be done. Uphold our Father's
teaching and watch how fast our Father's teachings lift us
up. May Allah bless us all.

PEACE . . . PEACE . . .
BROTHER A.M. MUHAMMAD

(Reprint From ALLAH IN MUHAMMAD SPEAKS . . . VOLUME 1-13 . . . 1/17/89)

SHABAZZ

Every so-called Negro is not Shabazz. We have black people here, in this country from all parts of the world. The black people who are descendants of slaves, whose fore parents were kidnapped and brought to America in slave-chains in the year 1555, these are the root of Shabazz. These are the tribe of God, or better known as the God tribe.

The white devil slave masters treated us like his animals and he bred us like he bred his animals. He had no sympathy for close family ties. The devils bred some of his negroes to think that they were better then their darker skinned brothers. Even today, a new breed of Uncle Tom Negroes have been regenerated.

We (Shabazz) are only those who will still have the true and living God, in our hearts and who have not forgotten the back breaking cotton fields, the sting of the whip, the rapes, the mutilations, the murders and more. To this very day, we Shabazz have not forgotten. We see it happening everyday of our lives.

The Uncle Toms hate us NEW WORLD SHABAZZ because we know the truth and tell the truth that God, is now here in person to free his modern-day slave and punish the slave masters and their made in America negroes, toms and traders against Allah and his God tribe Shabazz.

Allah says: "These dirty paid stool pigeons, back biters, hypocrites and toms are the first to be cast in the fire along with the devils. We only wait the hour."

Shabazz means perfection. According to the prophet of Allah, there are 144,000 of us here in the Wilderness of North America. May Allah bless and protect us all.

PEACE . . . PEACE . . .
BROTHER A.M. MUHAMMAD

(Reprint From ALLAH IN MUHAMMAD SPEAKS . . . VOLUME 1-8 . . . 7/17/87)

JESUS

IN THE NAME OF ALLAH IN THE PERSON OF MASTER PARD MUHAMMAD THE GREAT MAHDI. WE FOREVER PRAISE OUR FATHER THE MOST HONORABLE MR. ELIJAH MUHAMMAD FOR RESURRECTING US FROM THE DEAD!

Why was the President (King Herrod) so afraid of the New Born infant Jesus 2,000 years ago? What harm could a baby do to such a powerful government? It was not the physical power of baby Jesus that brought the armed forces against him. It was the Divine truth in the mind of Jesus that made him a ticking time bomb in the belly of King Herrod's wicked government.

Herrod knew, without a doubt that if Jesus be allowed to live he would teach his Father's (Allah God's) truth to the poor, needy, slave, those in prison houses and those on death row. Herrod knew the truth that Jesus taught would set the slaves free.

We, New World Nation of Islam are the infant of today. The President of this mighty Nation (America) is afraid of this small organization because we are born of the teachings of our Father the Most Honorable Mr. Elijah Muhammad, the Last God of the Old World and the First God of the New World Nation of Islam.

This modern-day King Herrod is aware that this truth, that the Black man is God, the White man is the devil, will free the Black slave from their master and will unite then unto a righteous Nation of Muslims under the leadership of the Great Mahdi, God in Person.

Allah is in Muhammad causing him to do God's will. The 'Mystique' of God was good for us in the past but Today God is in Person looking us straight in the face and asking you whose side are you on: Your own Black God Allah or are You on the side of the White Devil, the Beast, the Dragon, that old serpent called the Satan?

Read your Bible Revelations Chapter 12. This chapter is talking about You and Me and our fight against the devil.

The Dragon stands ready to attack the baby Nation but God comes to the aid of the infant. God armed the child and the baby Nation Wins the Divine battle. Allah is always on the side of those who fight against those who have attacked them. Allah does not help the aggressor.

The white devils attacked our Mothers and Fathers 400 years ago and took us away from our homeland in chains. They stripped us of everything and kept us captive slaves to this very day. God and his baby (the Son of Man) will win this fight for your freedom. The devil's time is up.

Jesus was not a white man, Jesus was a Black man. He did not teach Christianity he taught Islam. He did not die on the cross. He died at his own choosing. Jesus was taught mental telepathy at the age of 14. He knew what the devil's plans were as soon as they thought them. He chose to die after learning that the devils still had 2000 more years to live out their time. He wanted his life and death to be a sign for You and Me today, that if you are passive and do not fight back, the devil will lynch (crucify) you.

When Jesus was born he had no house, clothes, not even a crib to lay his head, but God sent Kings from the East to look out for him and to provide him with all he needed until he (Jesus) reached maturity. Allah has promised

Muhammad he would provide all the people and material that he will need to win Independence. The New World Nation of Islam is the baby Jesus of "Today".

Hurry and join your own Holy Nation of Islam under the guidance of Allah in Muhammad. Our Father the Most Honorable Mr. Elijah Muhammad said our Unity is greater than an Atomic Bomb.

PEACE . . . PEACE . . .
YOUR BROTHER A.M. MUHAMMAD

(Reprint From ALLAH IN MUHAMMAD SPEAKS . . . VOLUME 1-5 . . . 5/6/87)

IN THE NAME OF ALLAH
THE BENEFICENT, THE MERCIFUL

Dedicated To The Followers Of The Honorable Elijah Muhammad And The Independence Of The New World Nation Of Islam.

WAR

The Most Honorable Mr. Elijah Muhammad taught us that the separation of the so-called Negroes from their white slave masters, is a must.

It is the divine will of God that we be separated.

The civilized Nations of the earth look upon the so-called Negroes desire to stay in captivity, as chattel slaves, the worse kind of cowardice.

There is no respect, nowhere in this world for the so-called Negroes and there will be none until the so-called Negro unite with Muhammad and demand freedom and independence on some land to call our own.

The white man will never accept you as his equal. President Lincoln had no intentions of the Black Slave's social equality or freedom. He took the chains off the slave's hands and feet and put those chains on the slave's brain, by educating the so-called negroes into believing they are citizens of America.

Abraham Lincoln said, "I have no purpose to introduce political and social equality between the white and black races. There is a physical difference between the two, which in my judgement, will probably forever forbide living together upon the footing of perfect equality and in as much as it becomes a necessity that there must be a difference, I, as well as Judge Douglas, am in favor of the race to which I belong having <u>a superior portion</u>.

I am not, nor ever have been in favor of bringing about in any way the social and political equality of the white and Black races. I am not, nor ever have been, in favor of making voters or jurors of Negroes, nor of qualifying them to hold office, not to intermarry with White people." . . . First debate: August 21, 1858, widely publicized in 1960 by the White citizens council.

You must wake up Blackman and Black woman, there is no future for you under this white supremacist government.

America is angry because God has sent Muhammad to get you. Why shouldn't the great men and the fearless men of our Holy Tribe of Shabazz come to rescue the poor so-called negro from this modern-day slavery?

Allah says this day His Angels stand in ranks, and they will pay back to America twice what she has dealt to her poor slave.

Stand up my people. God has come for you. You are the greatest people that has ever walked on the face of this planet. Allah promises to make you the head of all the nations of the earth.

The white man knows that you are the chosen of God but he can't teach you that and expect you to continue to be his slave. He would be your slave if he revealed the truth to you.

William Faulkner (Nobel prize winner) said in 1932; "The Negro will endure. Their vices are vices aped from white men or that white men and bondage have taught them. And their virtues are endurance, pity, tolerance, forbearance, fidelity and love of their children."

Yes, that Whiteman is right. We have endured and we will continue to endure with the mercy and protection of Almighty God Allah, until victory and independence for our poor black people is won.

What fool would say that 50 million so-called Negroes should not have independence on some of this land to call their own?

Stand up Blackman, but if you are scared, then step aside and let Allah and Muhammad handle this.

Remember that the Blackman is God and the Whiteman is the devil, that will never change.

Read Holy Qur'an Chapter 11 Verses 120-123.

PEACE . . .PEACE . . .
YOUR BROTHER MUHAMMAD

(Reprint From ALLAH IN MUHAMMAD SPEAKS . . . VOLUME 1-6 . . . 5/10/87)

IN THE NAME OF ALLAH
THE BENEFICIENT, THE MERCIFUL

Dedicated To The Followers Of The Honorable Elijah Muhammad And The Independence Of The New World Nation Of Islam.

PEACE

Our Father the Most Honorable Mr. Elijah Muhammad to whom we forever Praise, taught us that the most valuable things in the universe are those that last forever.

Peace is the crown of life. It is God's gift to every creature. Babies are born with it, but we soon take peace from our children as we raise them to be other than Muslims.

There is no greater knowledge or a more important knowledge, than knowledge of Allah, the true and living God being a man and not a spook and is now present, judging this world.

When our understanding of Allah is Right, we realize that God and Peace are one. The first step is to come in contact with God or the human soul where He is manifest and receive divine guidance.

It is divine guidance that purifies the heart and keeps all other thoughts but that of the will of Allah from us.

The Honorable Mr. Elijah Muhammad taught us that there are many lessons before we learn to keep the peace. However, one of the quickest ways to learn the peace and keep the peace is by counting our blessings at least 5 times a day. Remember there is always someone in a worse situation than you.

We, Elijah Muslims, know that after waiting comes patience and after patience comes peace.

Once peace is acquired it never changes, it is everlasting.

We are moving in the opposite direction of all other civilizations. That is to say, we are after physical and spiritual perfection, which is the decrease of attachments and desires for this world. The less we want and are attached to, the more perfect is our peace.

Islam is not our religion; it is our way of life. The way we live is to attain perfect peace. Of course, we believe in Allah, God but we don't accept the idea of some spirit in the sky that no one knows or sees.

We, the tribe of Shabazz, are the family of God. He is real among us, not a spook. The original Blackman's history shows that whenever a major change took place, a Blackman possessed of God brought it about.

This day, Allah makes all things subservient to Muhammad. Master Fard (Gabriel, before he left) authorized Brother Muhammad to be in charge and responsible for this New World Nation of Islam. God Allah doesn't change his choice of a divine man once the die is set, it never changes.

This divine teaching comes from our Father the Most Honorable Mr. Elijah Muhammad, it is his cause. We believers effectuate his teachings by putting them into practice.

We forever thank Allah in the person of our Father the Honorable. Mr. Elijah Muhammad who raised from among us our Saviour Master Fard Muhammad, the Great Mahdi, the Crusher of the wicked.

Read Holy Qur'an, Chapter 11 Verses 120-123.

PEACE . . . PEACE . . .
YOUR BROTHER MUHAMMAD

(Reprint From ALLAH IN MUHAMMAD SPEAKS . . . Volume 1-9 . . . 8/17/87

In The Name Of Allah In Muhammad. We Forever Thank Our Father The Most Honorable Mr. Elijah Muhammad For His Divine Guidance Without Which (We) New World Nation Of Islam Couldn't Exist.

PEACE
PART III

How does a Muslim attain spiritual Perfection?

When you can hear the truth with a spiritual ear and see truth with a spiritual eye your faith and devotion grow strong. The greater the devotion the more you want to serve Allah.

He, Allah is the one in the mirror that looks right into you. He is looking into your very being. He knows what you think and the reasons behind everything you do. He is the reason you are never alone. He listens to you, he talks with you, and he always advises you of the right thing to do. When you are at those crucial points in life and it looks like you just can't go on, He is the One who picks you up, places you on his shoulders and carries you over the trial.

You know that it is Allah when what is said bears witness to the guidance given to Prophets and Scriptures of the past. Also, it serves our present situation and gives us a look at the future.

Our Father taught us that Allah is not limited in the ways in which He will reveal guidance to us. He will use any and everything to make us aware of the right direction. He will use even a rock (like the Black-Stone at Mecca) as a

70

sign but whatever He uses it is always backed up by scriptures.

The less you know about the scriptures the harder it is to verify God's word to you. That is why our Father said it is a Muslim's duty to read, write, believe in and study Scripture. There are four steps in becoming one with Allah or Perfection.

The first step is to be *resurrected* from the mentally dead state of being. Resurrection is waking up from mental death, not physical death. You are alive when you know that the Blackman is the original man, the father of civilization and the God who created the universe. You are alive when you know that the white man is the devil, the wicked and evil skunk of the planet earth. Not underground after you die, but right here and now face to face. We call this resurrection Spiritual Birth. Like babies in their birth fat surrounded by his own urine and waste; man, on his lowest level is animalistic and wasteful: smoking, drinking, gambling, drugs, stealing, lying, murder, rape, sinful and rebellion (surrounded by wrongs of his own choosing).

The second level is *conscious* stage. This is when we stand up and declare that Allah is One True and Living God and acknowledge and confess all our faults. Now the Muslim must begin to read and write. He must study Divine history (Scripture), knowledge of himself and Nation. Our Father made us (Believers) recite 112 divine questions and answers before we qualified for rank in the Nation of Islam. We learn to practice on the second level.

The third stage is *perfection*. It is at this level that the student Muslim learns that all things originate from Allah and that the highest aspiration is to make Allah his exclusive goal in life. He must rid himself of all attachments, family, friends, property and bad habits. His word becomes his bond. He does not allow hard trials or difficulties take him off the path to Allah and complete peace. The Muslim now knows that a life without Allah is no life at all. Our Father, the Most Honorable Mr. Elijah Muhammad taught Bro. Fard and myself to trust no one but Allah. Also that we are perfect when we can let Allah's will be done regardless of whom or what.

The fourth stage is the level in which the Muslim merges into *oneness* with Allah. After he learns to submit to Allah and those in authority and has practiced hearing and obeying from 23 to 25 years (There is an exception to this rule), Allah reveals to him his true identity and the plan He has for the Salvation of His Nation. When you know God, self and how you fit in Allah's Universal Plan, you are a living manifestation that Allah is one God begets not and not begotten. Also that everyone is born with a special job to do and only God can reveal that Divine identity. It is then and only then that a Muslim's life and death is all for Allah. He is in Allah and Allah is in him and none can duplicate the great work of one Divinely Chosen and Guided by Allah.

If you accept that I am an Apostle, then your reward is that of an Apostle. If you accept Me as a Prophet then your reward is that of a Prophet. If you accept that I am God then your reward is that of a God!

NEW WORLD NATION OF ISLAM is born out of the seed of our Father the Most Honorable Mr. Elijah Muhammad. He is the Lord of this world. He, Elijah, passed this divine Supreme Wisdom on to his two sons Fard Saviour and Ali Mahdi Muhammad. Our Father commissioned Bro. Fard to build the House of our Father's desire (New World) and after teaching us for 15 years He left. Master Fard Saviour commissioned General

Muhammad and after 26 years he left Brother Ali to complete that work.

Our Father's teaching will be as up to date many years from now, as it is today. Our Father taught us that righteousness is the Key. He instructed us to control our appetites and to take care of the ones who need it.

Only the foolish will refuse to believe what I am teaching you is the truth. Let me quote two European scientists. Albert Einstein (Scientist) said "Only a life lived for others is a life worthwhile. The true value of a human being is determined by the measures and the sense in which he has attained liberation from self."

Manly P. Hall, in his book Super Faculties and their Cultures pg. 28 says "Ancient wisdom the fourth highest plane in which man can function is called the mental world. This mental world is the mind body of the Solar God. The (ancient) mystery school, by means of four initiations, teach man how to function consciously in the four worlds of nature. In the fourth initiation, they teach him how to use that little area of consciousness, which he calls his mind as a vehicle by which he can function consciously within the mental body of the Grand Man. In other words, he is taught how to wander around in the mind of God. This may seem a very peculiar idea, and yet, the system of accomplishing this has been taught by the Egyptians, Chinese, Hindus, Chaldeans, etc. for thousands of years."

Today your poor Brother is teaching you pure Islam. THE BLACKMAN IS GOD and the white man is the Devil, not in the by and by after you die, but in reality here and now.

Hurry and help Me build the New World Nation of Islam.

PEACE . . . PEACE . . .
YOUR BROTHER, A.M. MUHAMMAD

(Reprint From ALLAH IN MUHAMMAD SPEAKS . . . VOLUME 1-19 . . . JULY 1989)

IN THE NAME OF ALLAH, THE MOST MERCIFUL . . .
PEACE, PEACE . . .

PSYCHIC SCIENCE

Allah's is the North, West, South, and East. He is all and all. WE are dependent upon Him, He doesn't need us. If we obey His guidance, it will cause us to live a good life. A life of righteousness.

How long we live or how healthy we exist depends on what we eat physically and mentally. You must understand that we are what we eat.

If we train ourselves to eat every three days, we will never be sick. If we read the Holy Qur'an at night and in the mornings, Allah will allow you to speak the truth to the hearts of men.

If you ate only once a week, you would soon notice that you know what's on the mind of others, also you will begin to know and see things happening before others see it. This is some of the psychic powers that we lost as civilization degenerated into sickness and death.

Thanks, thanks to Allah, for rescuing us from mental and physical slavery. As we learn the great discipline of the Gods, we'll become Gods. A God would not put poisonous food in his mouth. Nor would he feed garbage to his brain.

After you practice these divine attributes, people of great sensitivity towards truth will search you out and ask you to teach them how you got those Godly characteristics. You are obligated to teach them all the truth you know. The quickest way to learn and be blessed with great leadership of man, is to teach and practice what you preach.

Islam is the science of everything in life. Once we learn how to return to godhood, we must know the way to our sleeping brothers and sisters.

Our Father the Hon. Mr. Elijah Muhammad, who is the Last God of the Old World and the First God of the New World Nation of Islam, taught us that there is nothing more important to a Muslim then Prayer. He said ask Allah for whatever you want and he will give it to you.

So, Brother Ali Mahdi Muhammad, asked to be His number one follower. Our Lord Elijah gave your Brother Ali the name Ruh Al Ma Ani, December 1960. He sent A.M. Muhammad and some of his other good servants to school to learn to be our leader and teacher of Islam. Allah answers him who praises Him.

Today you have some people who do not like that your Bro. A.M. Muhammad teach and guide you into righteousness. But they could have had this job if they had prayed for it. But they prayed for other things in this world. Don't blame Muhammad and the believers for your short-sightedness.

If you want to be a leader, ask Allah for it. Remember the more physical food we eat the shorter we live. The more mental food we eat (of the truth) the longer we live. Your superior mental powers will return to you as you continue to pray, walk in the footsteps, and practice the guidance of God. To act like Him, is to Be Him.

Also, remember: to act like the devil, makes you a devil.

A true Muslim submits to Allah, and the truth only. He is faithful, trustworthy, dedicated and fearless of all but Allah. Pray for knowledge, wisdom and understanding.

PEACE . . . PEACE . . .
A.M. MUHAMMAD

(Reprint From ALLAH IN MUHAMMAD SPEAKS . . .VOLUME 1-10 . . . 9/17/87)

IN THE NAME OF ALLAH IN MUHAMMAD...

*** JUDGMENT AND FLYING SAUCERS ARE NO JOKE ***

Allah is the God of the universe. He, Allah, (the Blackman) created everything. Long before this part of the universe was made, we (the Gods) lived in other parts of the galaxies. We came to this part of our planet earth aboard a space craft that was powered by the sun's energy. That space ship could fly through the universe.

The planet earth has been an experimental place for the black gods. Allah wanted us to experience everything in life, so he created this planet to perfect our Islam. Life and death, heaven and hell, sickness and health, joy and sorrow. We the God tribe of Shabazz, have experienced it all and Allah, in person, has been right here with us every step of the way.

It is silly to think that we, here on this little planet, are the only people in the universe. There are seven inhabited planets in this solar system. Mars and the people of Mars were our satellite before we moved to this part of our solar system and created the planet earth. The Martian people are closest to our own physical appearance. They are black, slender and are an average of 10 feet tall.

Allah, God, created everything. We created the bird, so we too can fly, we created the fish, so we too can live in the water, we created the bear, so we too can hibernate, we created the snake, so we too can fast long periods without eating. In fact, we the gods don't need to eat or drink.

We made the food and water. We are not dependent on it. We did without it before we made it and we will do without it again.

According to Allah's word to me, we will systematically cut down on eating and drinking until we stop altogether. Of course there are other worlds like ours out there. Some of the UFO's are our alien brothers and protectors. They keep a close eye on our enemies and watch our progress.

These are the heavenly angels, the guardians from the sky, the Wheel within a Wheel, that the prophet Ezekiel saw coming down from heaven to perform God's will of saving the righteous and destroying the wicked.

The Blackman's Day is come. We are the gods of today and forever more. We will lead the way back to our Father's House, our home amongst the stars. Remember: We just live on this planet, but our home is the entire Universe.

PEACE . . . PEACE . . .
ALI MAHDI MUHAMMAD

(Reprint From ALLAH IN MUHAMMAD SPEAKS . . . Volume 1-18 . . . 11/17/88)

IN THE NAME OF ALLAH IN MUHAMMAD....
PEACE, PEACE.

JUDGMENT
By A.M. MUHAMMAD

Judgment means separation. It separates the wheat from the weeds, the righteous from the wicked, the blacks from the whites and God, from the devil.

The Whiteman is the oppressor of black people all over the planet earth. He, the devil has robbed and made himself rich by enslaving the black man, there must be a separation if the black man is to be free of white domination.

Judgment is when God declares the end of white supremacy. Judgment is divine revelation that put right against wrong, black against white, and God against devil.

Today God Allah stands in the congregation of the mighty, the awakened black gods here in America. He is calling you Black brothers and sisters to stand up and build your own black Nation under the guidance of Master Fard Muhammad, the Great Mahdi.

Judgment separates those who love the white devils from those who hate the devils. When you stand up for Allah and Muhammad, those who love the devils will hate you. Truth of the Whiteman turns parents against their own children, husbands against wives and brothers against sisters.

Judgment separates the righteous Muslim who submits to the truth of Allah, from the hog-eating, Christian, and alcohol-drinking negro, to a peaceful, happy, and upright healthy person.

God comes to separate us, not to integrate us among our enemies. The sheep must be separated from the goats.

Our Father (H.E.M.) says the time of our separation is now. Hurry and join unto your black Nation. The Judgment of America is at hand!

Remember, God is here to separate us. He will not integrate us among the same white devils who have destroyed us for more than 400 years. Only the fools, tools, and toms of the white man would tell you to integrate.

PEACE . . . PEACE . . .
SUPREME MINISTER OF ELIJAH MUHAMMAD

IN THE NAME OF ALLAH IN MUHAMMAD

FREE THE CAPTIVE BELIEVERS

Captive Believers must be delivered from Satan's prison houses. The white devils plan to destroy our black people by imprisonment of our young black males and the sterilization of our young black females (birth control pills) will fail. Putting us in prison by the hundreds and thousands has resulted in gathering us young aggressive blacks in one place so Allah in the Person of Master Fard Muhammad, the Great Mahdi, will have no problem in finding us. Also, because of these great teachings of the Hon. Mr. Elijah Muhammad, our young and beautiful black sisters are refusing to take those poisonous birth control pills.

The devil's plan will always fail, and Allah's plans are forever successful. It is Allah's plan to let our great men and our great black women stand up behind your brother, General Muhammad, and help him free our people from this modern-day slavery. We are the best at whatever we set our minds to do. We are living in a time when the truth will force you to accept it.

Allah says, "The first works of Master Fard Muhammad the Great Mahdi is to free the Captive Believers."

PEACE . . . PEACE . . .
YOUR BROTHER,
A.M. MUHAMMAD

"CLOSING"

In The Name Of Our Father The Most Honorable Mr. Elijah Muhammad, To Whom All The Praise Is Forever Due, And In The Name Of Our Lord Brother Ali Mahdi Muhammad, *The Great Mahdi*. We Pray To You, O' Allah, That This Work Is Pleasing To Thee . . .

"ALLAH IS THE GREATEST"

PEACE . . . PEACE . . .
Po Bro. Major. Jamil Ali Allah

IN THE NAME OF ALLAH, THE BENEFICIENT, THE MOST MERCIFUL

The following books are a must-read for us to get the proper understanding of our spiritual Father's message and teachings. The Honorable Elijah Muhammad left not one stone unturned in His message to us. It is on time and in time, 100% correct, but only a few were given the proper understanding. The following books keep you on the path of the Honorable Elijah Muhammad **written by The Honorable Mr. Elijah Muhammad:**

Supreme Wisdom Volume 1 $7.95	**Volume 2 $8.95**
Message To the Blackman Volume 1 $7.95	**$17.95**
How to Eat to Live - Volume 1 $12.95	**Volume 2 $13.95**
Our Saviour Has Arrived	**$14.95**
Fall of America	**$15.95**
Theology of Time	**$18.95**
The Flag of Islam	**$8.95**
Yakub: Father of Mankind	**$14.95**
True History of Master Fard Muhammad	**$14.95**
Black Stone: True History of Hon. Elijah Muhammad	**$22.95**
The Secrets of Freemasonry	**$7.95**
The Science of Time	**$7.95**
My People are Destroyed	**$12.95**
The Theology of Time - Subject Indexed	**$29.95**
The Theology of Time – Direct Transcript	**$18.95**
Mother Plane – UFO	**$7.95**
The God Science of Black Power	**$10.95**

Blood Bath: True Teachings of Malcom X	**$7.95**
Divine Sayings of the Hon. Elijah Muhammad Volumes 1-3	**$8.95**
A Plain Understanding of the Red Dragon	**$12.95**
The God -Tribe of Shabazz	**$14.95**
Dissatisfaction Between Black & White	**$13.95**
Christianity vs. Islam	**$11.95**
True History of Jesus', Birth, Death	**$10.95**
True History of Honorable Elijah Muhammad	**$29.95**
100 Answers To The Most Uncommon 100 Questions	**$11.95**
Foundation Years of Elijah Muhammad	**$24.95**
History of the Nation of Islam Interview	**$11.95**
Holy Qur'an By Maulana Muhammad Ali	**$29.95**

Also Read the Keys to the proper understanding of our Father's teachings of: The Two Histories of Moses, The Two Histories of Jesus, the Two Histories of Prophet Muhammad and the Two Histories of Master Fard Muhammad. All of these histories can be found in the books of the Honorable Mr. Elijah Muhammad.

The Following Titles Are by Ali Mahdi Muhammad:

1. Al Fard (The Dawn) by A. M. Muhammad $14.95
2. Knowledge of The Gods by A. M. Muhammad $14.95
3. Elijah Muhamad's New World Nation of Islam $14.95

**The Future Master Fard Muhammad
by Elijah Muhammad**   **$12.95**

To place your order send orders to:

New World Nation of Islam
P.0. Box 8466
Newark, NJ 07108

Add price of book and $6.95 shipping/handling of 1st book $2.50 for each additional book.

Ingram Content Group UK Ltd.
Milton Keynes UK
UKHW020916190723
425423UK00001B/58